The Green Peafowl

Written by Han Lianxian, Yang Xing, and Chen Jinsou   Illustrated by Bai Song and Sun Heyu

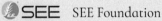

Preface

The Southwest Project Center of the Alashan Society of Entrepreneurs & Ecology (SEE) initiated a program in 2013 for biodiversity conservation of the alpine forests in China's mountainous Southwest. Named SEE Noah's Ark, it is financed by the SEE Foundation in Beijing. Multiple conservation projects have been implemented by working with various stakeholders to protect endangered and rare species of flora and fauna, especially those with extremely small populations. It adopts solutions inspired by nature and advocates participation by the community, encouraging protection and the sustainable use of local biological resources.

The stories in the SEE book series: *The Asian Elephant*, *The Yunnan Snub-Nosed Monkey*, *The Green Peafowl*, *The Fish of the Jinsha River*, and *The Himalayan Honeybee*, all come from true experiences of front-line rangers and locals in conservation action. They are incredible. For both nature's characters and the people in the story, their connection to the native land and affection towards each other is rarely heard and miraculous in their own way. We then came up with a proposal to compile these lovely stories in a picture book to all our friends who have supported SEE conservation projects. They can be linked to real characters from dense woods and remote mountains, where heart touching stories occurred due to their generous support.

This picture book series is a group of works by conservation workers, scientists, sociologists, writers, and artists. The characters, environment, and neighboring creatures have all been carefully selected from real situations in our projects. In addition, explanatory notes of conservation are made to enrich the reading experience. We hope you enjoy it!

We extend our respects to those who have worked so hard to conserve their natural homeland, as well as to the SEE members and public who give donations to support these projects. These volumes are our gifts for the United Nations Biodiversity Conference COP15 held in Kunming.

XIAO JIN
Secretary of the SEE's Southwest Project Center
Chairperson of the SEE Noah's Ark Committee
June 2021

Data File: Green Peafowl

Name in Chinese	绿孔雀 (LÜKONGQUE)
Name in English	Green peafowl
Alternate Names	Java peacock, Vietnamese bird, Dragon Bird
Latin Name	*Pavo muticus*
Kingdom	Animalia
Phylum	Chordata
Subphylum	Vertebrata
Class	Aves
Subclass	Neornithes
Order	Galliformes

Family	Phasianidae
Subfamily	Peacock
Genus	*Pavo*
Species	*P. muticus*
Distribution	Cambodia, China, Indonesia, Laos, Burma, Thailand, Vietnam
Authorship	Linnaeus, 1766 Linnaeus, 1766
Conservation Status	(EN) IUCN Endangered

Prefectural-level City/ Autonomous Province	County/ District	Nature Reserve
Yuxi	Yuanjiang	Yunnan Yuanjiang National Nature Reserve
Yuxi	Yuanjiang	Yubaiding Farm Nature Reserve
Yuxi	Yuanjiang	Green Peafowl Yaocun Community Nature Reserve, Zhelong Township
Yuxi	Yuanjiang	Green Peafowl Xiaoyang Nature Reserve, Zhelong Township
Yuxi	Yuanjiang	Green Peafowl Nature Reserve, Laochang Township
Yuxi	Yuanjiang	Green Peafowl Nature Reserve, Xinhua Township
Yuxi	Eshan	Green Peafowl Yale Community Nature Reserve, Fuliangmeng Township
Chuxiong Yi Autonomous Prefecture	Chuxiong	Konglong River Nature Reserve

A-Mi is a little girl of Yi ethnicity. She is 12 years old, and she lives in Phoenix Tweeting Village on the bank of the Shiyang River, which flows from the upper reaches of the Hong River in Yunnan.

One early morning in July, she and her dad, A-Bu, climbed up the mountain to look for mushrooms. There in the woods, they spotted an enormous bird. There it was – hiding in the shrubs, covered with kingfisher blue plumage. When it saw them coming, it started to flee, hobbling and limping. Having only made a few steps, it just squatted on the ground and could not move anymore.

"That's the green peafowl," Dad said, "It's the green phoenix in our mountains."

A-Mi had never seen such a creature before. The peafowl's sparkling blue feathers made her think to herself: this is the most beautiful bird in the forest. But its eyes express much pain. This is what A-Mi thought in her heart. "Daddy, we have to help it!" she said, turning to A-Bu.

The Green Peafowl

The Green Peafowl is the largest species of pheasant in China. At present, it can be found only in central and southern Yunnan with a population of under 600. It is in Grade-I for conservation on the List of Wildlife for Special State Protection. It is classified as a threatened species on the IUCN (International Union for Conservation of Nature) Red List of Threatened Species (2013).

A-Bu placed the wounded peafowl carefully into his wicker basket. A-Mi followed her father back to the village. She heard a few gentle groans coming from the peafowl in the basket. They then informed the village's forestry station as soon as they were back home.

Domestic chicken

She brought over some grains and water that she fed her chicks. She put them on the ground for the peafowl to peck at. But they didn't have any idea how they would treat the wound …

The Green Peafowl

The green peafowl belongs to the Phasianidae Family under the Galliformes Order. It is the prototype of the divine "phoenix" bird in traditional Chinese culture, and has been regarded as "the Lord of Birds" since ancient times. Commonly known as the "Green Phoenix" or "Emerald Chicken," an honorific archway named "Emerald Chicken Archway" was built and is located in the center of Kunming City.

Pheasant expert Luo Ya, carrying out research work on peafowl conservation on the bank of the Shiyang River, hurried to A-Mi's home as soon as he got the news.

He cleaned and healed the peafowl's wound and gave A-Bu and A-Mi some instructions to care for the bird. In the following days, as soon as he finished his field-work, Luo Ya always headed over to check on the peafowl's recovery.

Luo Ya passed over some scientific knowledge to A-Mi and told her interesting stories about green peafowls in the forest. In spring, when the green peafowls start a loud and clear "A-woo-ao" in the woods, it is the courtship call for the green peacocks (male) during the breeding season.

The Green Peafowl

The green peafowls usually make their habitats in tropical or subtropical evergreen broad-leaved forests or mixed forests below 2,000 meters in elevation. At night they rest on the flatter branches of tall trees. Their preferable habitats are forests and valleys with running streams. They especially like to forage in both the sand and the open forest, where fruits and berries are plentiful.

The wound on the peafowl's leg gradually healed up. It stood up and started to walk around the courtyard, pecking on the bits of corn and peas that A-Mi threw on the ground.

Luo Ya told A-Mi: "It has almost recovered. Now we've got to send it back to the mountain forest, back to its companions."

Luo Ya attached a numbered band to the peafowl's left leg. He said, "next time we see it, we'll recognize it straight away."

The Green Peafowl

At breeding sites, overwintering sites or rest sites of migrating birds, scientists capture birds and attach bandings, an individually numbered metal ring or coloured tag, inscribed with the address of the National Bird Banding Center on the tarsus or lower leg of the bird. The bird is then released. The tag can provide additional information should it be observed or caught and released once again. This is one of the means of studying birds and marking their individual identification. Usually, a bright colored tag or metal ring is used.

Noah's Ark
Community Nature
Reserve for Green
Peafowl Habitat

It's 2017, and Phoenix Tweeting Village has built a Nature Reserve for the community to protect the green peafowls. A-Bu is appointed to the patrol squad.

"It's the pride of our village that these endangered peafowls can live and continue their breeding in the forests behind our village," he said to A-Mi. "Those trees are the peafowls' home: we shouldn't go in there to pick mushrooms or graze our sheep during their incubating season. Just let them lay eggs and raise their baby chicks in peace. To help increase their numbers is the only way they can survive here in the long run."

A-Bu often went out and spread the same message to villagers. He also passed the words to family relatives and guests who were visiting.

The Green Peafowl

The Community Nature Reserve for Wildlife is a natural conservation practice, comprising joint efforts from local communities, CSOs (Civil society organizations) and government authorities. The protection targets rare and endangered wild animals and their habitats beyond the government-established nature reserves.

A-Mi couldn't forget the green peafowl after it was released. In winter, she signed up as a volunteer for the patrol squad.

Luo Ya and his colleagues came over to train the volunteers before they headed into the mountains. A-Mi and her dad learned how to install an infra-red camera and how to write their patrol notes. They learned a lot about wild animals and the green peafowl as well.

The Green Peafowl

Journal notes include: time, weather, patrol route, patrol personnel, and new animals and plants encountered on patrol, including area spotted, marks and excreta, direction of sounds heard and slope information etc.

During the winter vacation in January, A-Mi and her father went back into the mountains to begin their patrol. They followed a small trail through the forests, hiking most of the day in the mountain. Father A-Bu carried a rucksack packed with peas and corn. They threw a handful on the ground every time they got to a place where peafowls would often go or dig for food.

A-Bu told his daughter: Winter is the dry season in the Ailao Mountains. The weather is heating up with little rain. There have been quite a few years of continued drought. There are not a lot of fruits in the woods for the peafowls. We have to provide some supplements to stop them from going hungry. The only way females can prepare well for breeding season in spring is by having enough food in the winter.

A peafowl's favorite foods:

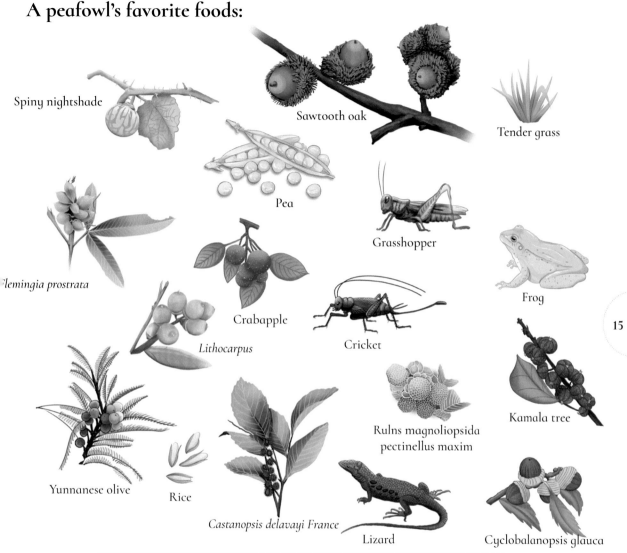

Spiny nightshade

Sawtooth oak

Tender grass

Pea

Grasshopper

Flemingia prostrata

Crabapple

Frog

Lithocarpus

Cricket

Kamala tree

Rulns magnoliopsida
pectinellus maxim

Yunnanese olive

Rice

Castanopsis delavayi France

Lizard

Cyclobalanopsis glauca

The Green Peafowl

The Chinese Green Peafowl is omnivorous and eats mostly seeds, worms, and wild fruits. But its forests nowadays have been mostly reclaimed and covered with tobacco, sugarcanes, walnuts, and sugar-sweet oranges by residents nearby. It resulted in habitat shrinkage or even disappearance. Peafowls in the nearby forests often go to agricultural fields in groups to search for food and that would damage the farmers' crops and reduce productivity. Another threat comes from seeds covered with pesticides. If the green peafowls eat these poisoned seeds, they may suffer fatalities.

Early every morning in February, A-Mi heard the peafowl's high-pitched singing and echoes in the forest. For their patrol, she and dad would switch out memory cards from infra-red cameras and change batteries. They'd bring them back to Luo Ya who examined each photo on his laptop.

The Green Peafowl!

It is the mating and breeding season of the Green Peafowls between February and June every year. Peafowls will meet in groups, hold their ground and claim their mating position with cries. To make a better display in front of the females, the male will show off his masculine charm. In order to win their hearts, the male peafowl works hard at unfolding its tail feathers when performing mating dances. During courtship, the male opens his plumage for a long time, attracting the female with gorgeous feathers and speckled pattern. This should encourage the female to mate with him!

Chinese goral

Some footage drew A-Mi's attention: the sight of a male green peafowl unfolding his tail and displaying his plumage. Almost at the same time, she and Luo Ya realized this one was the one they'd rescued and banded. He valiantly shook his beautiful plumage. Around him were four females looking for food, having fun, and chirping at each other. There was almost too much to take in for the male. He twisted his body left and right, unsure which lady he should turn his plumage towards. And sometimes he shook his tail quickly and made his feathers rustle, a rapid vibrating sound caught their attention. A-Mi plays the recording over and over and has watched it countless times.

The Green Peafowl

It is common behaviour for a male green peafowl to flaunt its tail. In the early stage of breeding, the colour of a male tail feather is especially gorgeous. The male birds often erect the tail, splattering vertically and expanding as a fan. They swing around in front of the female birds, and constantly shake valiantly. The tail feathers rub against each other, making a strange and rustling "sha-sha-sha" sound. The display could last longer than 10 or even 12 minutes. The male green peafowl sends a message to the female in this way that he is healthy and strong. Because he has enough food and does not lack nutrition, the feather is very bright and dazzling. Because of its strong body, the fanned tail screen could stand for a long time. Mating with a healthy male ensures baby peafowls will get their excellent genes. The more stunning the tail feather and the longer the display, the more the male green peafowl will be favored by females.

The Chinese green peafowl is polygamous, with a family formed with one male and at least two females. In the breeding season in February and March, under normal circumstances, a female should lay between 4–6 eggs each year. Incubation lasts about 27–30 days and each time around two to four will hatch successfully.

The Green Peafowl

In March, Luo Ya returned to collect the infra-red camera again. A-Mi was quite disappointed that there were not crowds of peafowls, just occasionally a male or youngster out foraging. Luo Ya told her that the females had probably hidden themselves to lay eggs.

With the infra-red camera photos, Luo Ya taught A-Mi how to tell color markings on the cheek and how to make files for each individual peafowl.

Silver pheasant

In May, a female appeared in the infra-red shot. A-Mi caught sight of four chicks with brownish feathers on which were yellowish dots. On their head stood an upright crown. They took little broken footsteps, closely following behind mother, with her head high.

Chicks cannot run fast or fly. With brownish dots on their feathers, they can not be easily spotted by predators and are well disguised. At age one, the peafowl will resemble its mother and striking colours have begun to emerge on the necks of males. At two, an adolescent resembles an adult. At three-year-old, the coloration is the same as adults, with males beginning to develop a tail in glorious colors.

The Green Peafowl

Wild boar

Silver pheasant

Luo Ya explained how the chick feathers would look just as lovely as mom's and dad's when they grew up. He and A-Mi made files for the mother and new borns, giving them all names. "Four new peafowl babies added to the forest this year!" announced Luo Ya.

A-Mi sketched a peafowl with her color pencils. Everybody loved her drawing. The Nature Reserve Community got it printed onto their New Year's poster, on the door for each village home.

Now, everybody around has heard about the beautiful peafowls living in the mountain forests behind their villages. The most gorgeous one among them is the very same peafowl that A-Mi and her dad rescued and sent back to the woods.

The Green Peafowl

An "umbrella species" is a species well-known among the public, whose habitat may cover the habitat needs of other species. The protection of an umbrella species could help protect other species effectively. The green peafowl is such a species in rainforest and mixed coniferous forest environments. When its habitat in forests along river valleys is conserved well and when its population increases, other species living in the protected forest will also benefit.

About the Authors

Han Lianxian (male, Han Chinese) received his master's degree from the Kunming Institute of Zoology in 1985. After that, he stayed at the Institute and engaged in research on bird classification, fauna, and Conservation Biology. He participated in the writing of The Avifauna of Yunnan China, The Phasianidae in China: Lady Amherst's pheasant, Rare and endangered wild chickens in China, etc. He taught and conducted research on ornithology and nature reserve management at Southwest Forestry University from 1997 to 2015 when he retired. He is the secretary-general of the Third Council of Yunnan Wildlife Conservation Association, a member of the Species Survival Committee of the International Union for Conservation of Nature (IUCN SSC), a member of the Pheasant Expert working group, and a member of Yunnan Nature Reserve Evaluation Committee.

Yang Xing became interested in the green peafowl when he was rafting in the Shiyang River in 2010 and saw these beautiful animals on the banks. Since then, he began studying and collecting information on the green peafowl's distribution and habitat. In 2015, he started organizing activities such as bird watching, bird photographing, and bird festivals among bird lovers. In 2017, he established the Yuxi Birdwatching Club and participated in the execution of the SEE Noah's Ark Green Peafowl's Habitat Conservation Project. In 2020, he participated in the investigation of green peafowl's habitat in the middle and upper reaches of the Yuanjiang River.

Chen Jinsou graduated from the tailing's engineering and management department at Kunming Metallurgy College in 2013. He joined the SEE Project Center in 2018 and engaged in green peafowl and Asian elephant protection works.

About the Illustrators

Bai Song has a Master's degree in engineering and has engaged in art education work for many years. She is now vice president and professional leader of Yunnan Light and Textile Industry Vocational Collage. She has edited and published two national planning textbooks, one jewelry major series teaching material for vocational institutes, and many educational, teaching, and research-related papers in relevant academic journals.

Sun Heyu received her master's degree in the art of design from Yunnan Arts University. She is now an assistant professor in the department and vice president and professional leader at the Yunnan Vocational College of Culture and Arts. She has held and participated in multiple research projects and published many papers in authoritative journals.

SEE Noah's Ark Biodiversity Conservation Book Series

SEE: The Green Peafowl

Written by Han Lianxian, Yang Xing, and Chen Jinsou
Illustrated by Bai Song and Sun Heyu

First published in 2023 by Royal Collins Publishing Group Inc.
Groupe Publication Royal Collins Inc.
BKM Royalcollins Publishers Private Limited

Headquarters: 550-555 boul. René-Lévesque O Montréal (Québec) H2Z1B1 Canada
India office: 805 Hemkunt House, 8th Floor, Rajendra Place, New Delhi 110 008

Original Edition © Yunnan Science & Technology Press Co., Ltd.

ISBN: 978-1-4878-1083-2

To find out more about our publications, please visit www.royalcollins.com.